MW01470301

THIS NOTEBOOK
BELONGS TO:

Made in the USA
Columbia, SC
20 January 2025

52174586R00067